Iron

by George Capaccio

Table of Contents

Pictures To Think About	i
Words To Think About	iii
Introduction	2
Chapter 1 The Nature of Iron	4
Chapter 2 Where Iron Is Found	10
Chapter 3 The Uses of Iron	16
Chapter 4 Iron and Steel	22
Conclusion	29
Solve This Answers	30
Glossary	31
Index	32

Pictures To Think About

Iron

Words To Think About

Characteristics
- mixture
- has two or more elements
- ?

Examples
- water
- hematite
- ?

compound

What do you think the word **compound** means?

mineral

What do you think the word **mineral** means?

What are some facts about **minerals**?
- 4,000 in all
- ?
- make up the rocks on Earth

What are some **minerals**?
- silver
- ?
- gold

Read for More Clues
bloom, page 17
compound, page 5
mineral, page 6

bloom

What do you think the word **bloom** means in this book?

Meaning 1
to produce or yield flowers
(verb)

Meaning 2
a soft, partly melted lump of iron
(noun)

Meaning 3
a powdery coating on fruit or leaves
(noun)

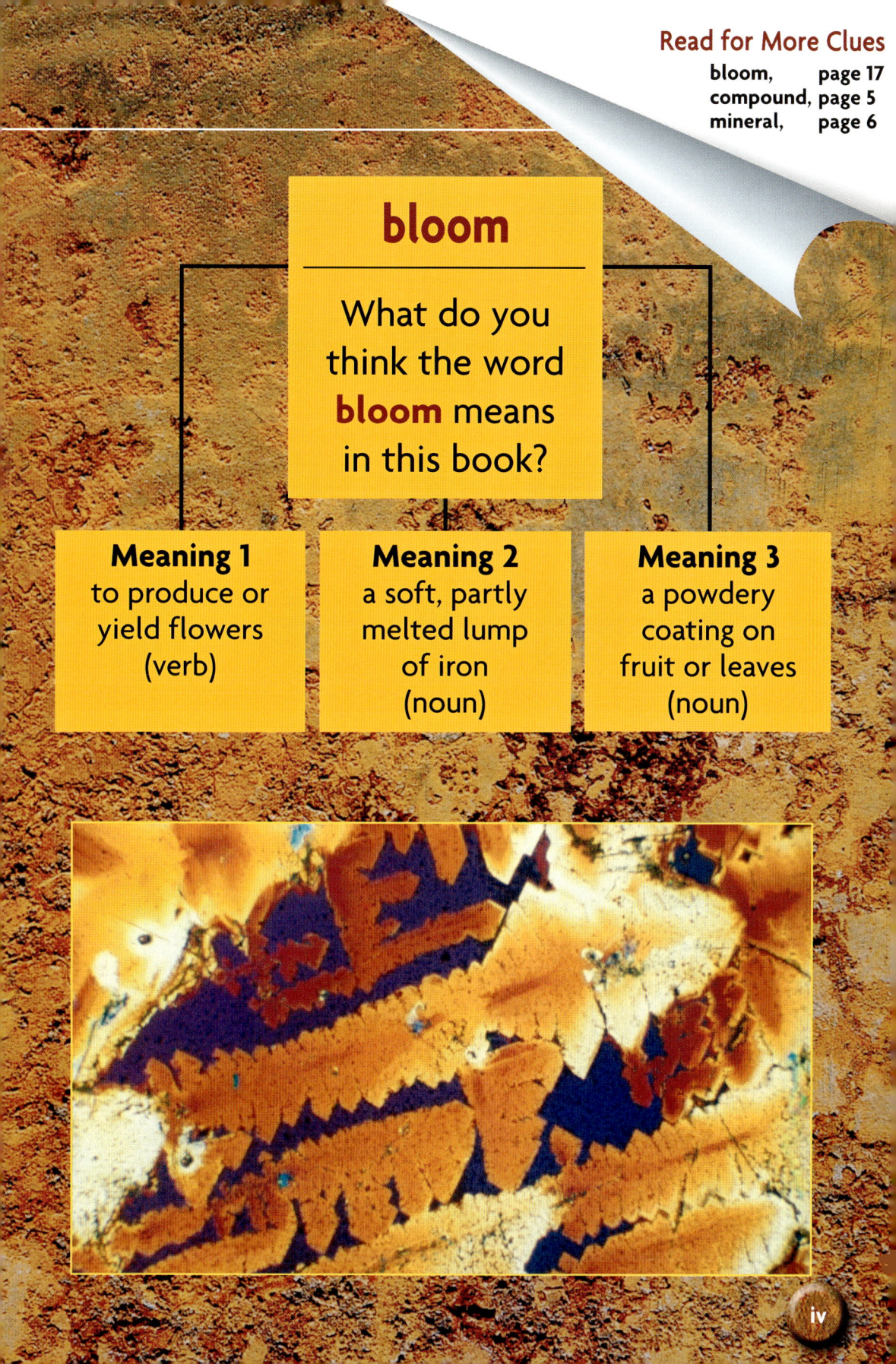

iv

Introduction

▲ Iron is used to make many different products.

People have used iron for about 5,000 years. At first, iron was hard to find. People thought iron was worth more than gold. People made jewelry and weapons with iron. It was hard to work with. In time, people found ways to melt iron. People started to mine iron. Iron became more common. People began to use it to make everyday items.

Today, iron is used to make cars, buildings, and bridges. Iron is also used to make cans and computers.

In this book you will read about iron. You will learn all about this **element** (EH-luh-mihnt). An element is a basic material. It cannot be broken down into something simpler.

You will find out why we call iron "a metal for the ages." You will learn about iron's **properties** (PRAH-puhr-teez), or features.

You will see from where iron comes. You will also see how iron has changed the world.

▼ **The Eiffel Tower is made completely of iron.**

CHAPTER 1

The Nature of Iron

Many of the objects you use every day are made of iron. Look around you. Computers and CD players contain iron. Videotapes have iron, too. Buses and cars also contain iron. Shopping malls, stores, schools, and tall buildings are made with iron. Pots, pans, and cans are made of iron, too.

◀ Objects made of iron are all around us.

HISTORICAL PERSPECTIVE

Long ago, many farm tools were made out of iron. The iron plow helped farmers produce more food. It made their work easier. Today, steel is used in modern farm equipment, such as threshers and tractors.

24 Cr	25 Mn	26 Fe	27 Co	28 Ni	29 Cu
42 Mo	43 Tc	44 Ru	45 Rh	46 Pd	47 Ag
74 W	75 Re	76 Os	77 Ir	78 Pt	79 Au
106 Sg	107 Ns	108 Hs	109 Mt	110 110	111 111

◀ The Periodic Table shows the elements that scientists have found in nature or have created in laboratories. Each element has its own symbol. The symbol for iron is Fe. Find iron in this section of the table.

Iron is an element. It is one of the most common elements on Earth. Pure iron is a soft, silvery gray metal. Pure iron is rare. Iron is normally found with other elements. A mixture of two or more elements is called a **compound**.

Hematite (HEE-muh-tite) is an iron compound. Magnetite (MAG-nuh-tite) is also an iron compound. Most iron comes from these compounds.

Iron is easy to find. Objects made from iron are strong. They last a long time. That is why we use iron to make so many things.

◀ Iron compounds are often black or reddish-brown.

CHAPTER 1

What's So Special About Iron?

Iron is a **mineral** (MIH-nuh-ruhl). Earth has about 4,000 minerals. Minerals form all of the rocks on Earth. Gold and diamonds are minerals.

Iron has special properties. Heat and electricity flow through iron. Iron is **malleable** (MA-lee-uh-buhl). That means it can bend. Workers can also hammer iron into different shapes. Iron bends at room temperature without breaking. At high temperatures, iron melts. Liquid iron can be poured into different molds.

Iron is also magnetic. Iron can be made into magnets. How do magnets work? Magnets have two ends. The ends are called poles.

Each magnet has a north and south pole. Take two magnets. Put the same ends together. The magnets will repel. They will move away from each other. Now place the different ends together. The magnets will move toward each other. The rule of magnets is "opposites attract."

Compasses have iron magnets. People use compasses to find which way is north. A compass needle always points north. Why? Because Earth's core is made of iron. Earth is like a giant magnet with north and south poles. That is how compasses know which way is north.

It's a Fact
Iron is one of three metals that are magnetic. Cobalt and nickel are the other two. Iron is the most magnetic of the three.

THE NATURE OF IRON

▼ Iron magnets can do everything from picking up paper clips to lifting heavy loads of scrap metal.

✔ POINT   PICTURE IT

Use the information about magnets to draw a diagram. Then use your diagram to explain to a partner how magnets work.

CHAPTER 1

▲ Even in the digital age, magnetic tape is still used in many products.

Iron is highly reactive. It easily combines with other elements. Mix iron with oxygen and you get iron oxide. Many iron oxide compounds are useful. Paints contain a type of iron oxide. That same oxide is also used in making videotapes. Magnetized bits in the iron oxide record sounds and images. Magnetic strips on bank cards also have iron oxide. The iron in each strip holds a person's bank account number. The strip lets people pay for things at stores. It also lets people get money at ATMs.

THE NATURE OF IRON

Iron can also make compounds that are not useful. Rust is a type of iron oxide. It has both iron and oxygen. Things made of iron will rust if they are not protected. That is why you should not leave iron outside when it rains or snows.

Another way to protect iron is to paint it. Or you can cover iron with another element, like zinc. Stainless steel is a form of iron. Stainless steel does not rust. That is because it is made with chromium (KROH-mee-um). This element stops the steel from rusting.

EVERYDAY SCIENCE

Beach sand sometimes contains fine black grains of sand. Often these are bits of magnetite, an iron compound. How can you find out if it's magnetite? Try using a magnet. If the magnet picks up the black sand, you can be pretty sure it's magnetite.

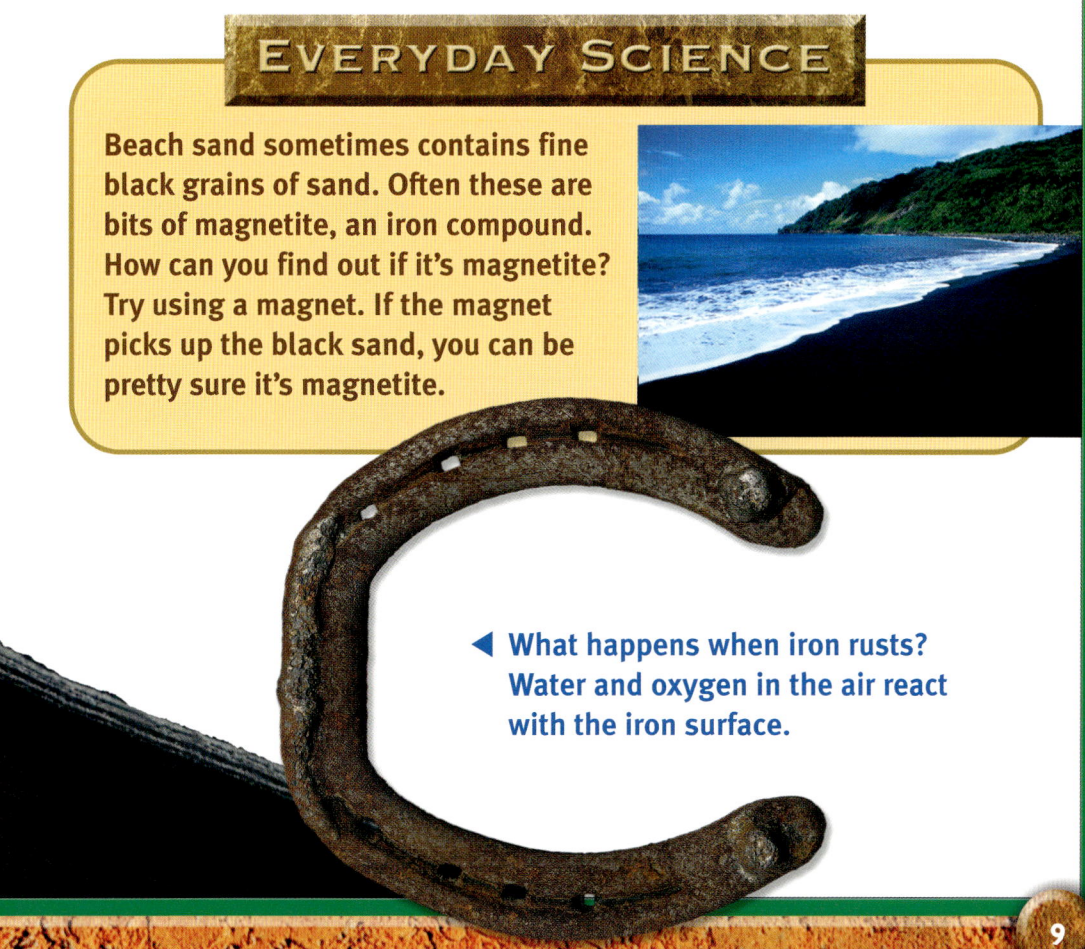

◀ What happens when iron rusts? Water and oxygen in the air react with the iron surface.

CHAPTER 2

Where Iron Is Found

Earth has four layers. The crust is the top layer of Earth. The **mantle** (MAN-tuhl) is the layer below the crust. About five percent of Earth's crust is iron. The mantle has a lot of iron. It also has other minerals.

Earth's inner core is about the size of the moon. Most scientists think that the inner core is solid iron. The outer core is the size of Mars. It is ninety percent **molten** (MOHL-tuhn) iron. Molten means melted.

How does iron get from the core to the crust? Read on to find out.

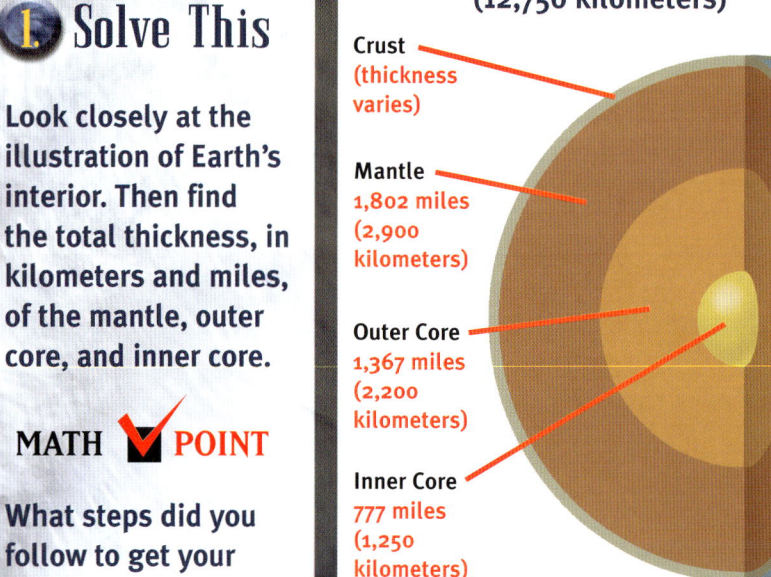

Cross Section of Earth
Total diameter: 7,922 miles (12,750 kilometers)

Crust (thickness varies)

Mantle
1,802 miles
(2,900 kilometers)

Outer Core
1,367 miles
(2,200 kilometers)

Inner Core
777 miles
(1,250 kilometers)

1. Solve This

Look closely at the illustration of Earth's interior. Then find the total thickness, in kilometers and miles, of the mantle, outer core, and inner core.

MATH ✔ POINT

What steps did you follow to get your answer?

Molten iron bubbles up from Earth's outer core. It passes through the mantle. Then it cools. It forms rocks in the crust. Most iron is found in rocks with other minerals. A rock with iron in it is called **ore**. Hematite is an iron ore. Hematite is reddish-black. Magnetite is also an iron ore. It is a black rock. It is also highly magnetic.

People find iron ore all over the world. Earth has as many as 800 billion tons of iron ore. Russia, Brazil, and China produce the most iron. Australia, India, and the United States also make a lot of iron.

CAREERS

Geologist

A geologist is a scientist who studies the materials that make up Earth. A mining geologist looks for minerals to make new kinds of metals. An environmental geologist explores ways to dispose of toxic wastes or protect natural resources. Geologists work in colleges and universities. They also work for private companies and for the government.

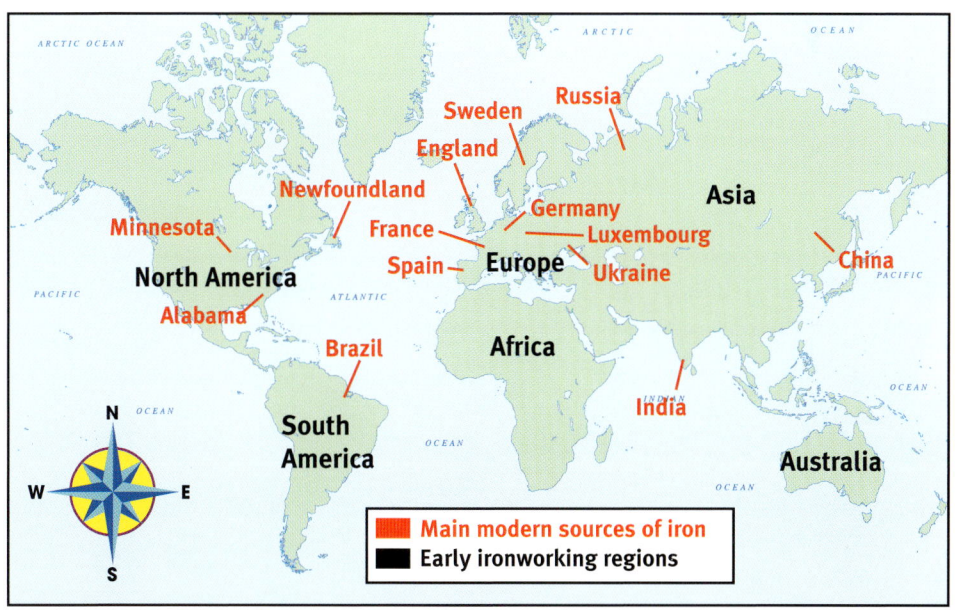

CHAPTER 2

▲ Meteor Crater in Arizona is nearly 1 mile (1.6 kilometers) wide and about 590 feet (179.8 meters) deep. The crater was created between 20,000 and 50,000 years ago when a meteorite hit Earth.

2. Solve This

Meteor Crater has a diameter of 80 feet (24.4 meters). What is the circumference of the crater?

MATH ✓ POINT

Is your answer reasonable? Why or why not?

Meteorites

Iron is also found in **meteorites** (MEE-tee-uh-ryts). These rocks from space sometimes hit Earth. Five billion years ago, many meteorites hit Earth.

The meteorites released a large amount of energy. The energy heated the planet. The meteorites also held large amounts of iron. This iron sank down into Earth's core.

WHERE IRON IS FOUND

Forms of Meteorites

Meteorites come in many types. Iron meteorites are made mostly of iron. Some scientists believe they were formed in the cores of other planets. Other scientists think that they were formed by exploding stars. Iron meteorites are heavier than most rocks found on Earth.

The first iron tools were probably made from iron meteorites. How did people find them? The meteorites fell from the sky. People might have seen them fall. People long ago called meteorites "metal from heaven."

▼ The largest known meteorite weighs about 121,000 pounds (54,884 kilograms). It was found in the African country of Namibia.

The Planet Mars

Iron is also found on Mars. We call Mars the "red planet." That is because Mars is red. It is red because rust, or iron oxide, covers much of its surface. The soil on Mars is about five to fourteen percent iron oxide. The planet also has a lot of iron ore. Scientists think about how to use the iron ore on Mars.

▼ This photo is a wide view of the surface of Mars. It was taken by an unmanned exploration vehicle, or rover. It shows the red surface.

In My Opinion

Scientists were very excited to find large amounts of hematite on Mars. This iron oxide usually forms on Earth in a watery environment like a lake or river. So some scientists thought that the presence of hematite could mean there was once water on Mars. This suggested that life may have existed on Mars. But scientists still do not know for sure.

WHERE IRON IS FOUND

One idea is to set up a small factory on Mars. The factory would make iron from the soil. Astronauts would use a process that the ancient Romans used. The process is called smelting. Smelting is when you melt iron ore and take out the iron. The iron could then be used to make machines and buildings. Then one day, humans could live and work on Mars.

▲ On January 24, 2004, *Opportunity*, an unmanned rover, landed on an area of Mars called Meridiani Planum. Mission planners picked this area because it contains a great deal of hematite.

CHAPTER 3

The Uses of Iron

Long ago, iron was hard to find. It took a long time to make things out of iron. The first ironworkers used iron they found in meteorites. They made jewelry and weapons from the iron. The weapons were just for show. The weapons were not used in battles.

People used mainly copper and bronze for tools. Bronze is an **alloy** (A-loy). An alloy is a mixture of two or more metals. Bronze is made of tin and copper. When it became hard to get tin, people turned to iron. They learned how to make iron from iron ore.

3. Solve This

The table on this page shows the melting points of different metals. Using either Celsius or Fahrenheit temperatures, make a line graph that plots the order of the melting points from the lowest to the highest.

MATH  POINT

If you rounded the ones digits in this problem, would your graph look the same? What if you rounded the thousands digits?

MELTING POINTS OF DIFFERENT METALS

Metal	Melting Point (Celsius)	Melting Point (Fahrenheit)
Aluminum	660	1,220
Gold	1,063	1,946
Iron	1,539	2,802
Lead	327	621
Silver	961	1,761

▲ Old-fashioned bloomery furnaces were once common in many parts of the world. Blacksmiths hammered the blooms to push out any impurities.

It's a Fact

Wrought iron was the main form of iron used into the 19th century. Wrought iron was black. That is why ironworkers were called blacksmiths.

Ironworkers still could not completely melt the iron. Their fires were not hot enough. The best they could do was make lumps of partly melted iron. The lumps were called **blooms**.

Blacksmiths reheated each bloom. When a bloom was red-hot, it was hammered into different shapes. This type of iron was called wrought iron.

CHAPTER 3

Early ironworkers knew about iron. But they did not know about carbon. Carbon could change iron. Charcoal is rich in carbon. The right amount of carbon will lower the melting point of iron.

In time, workers learned this trick. They added more charcoal to their fires. The iron melted faster. It became a liquid. The workers poured the liquid iron into molds. The result was cast iron.

The Age of Iron Begins

Over time, iron began to change people's lives. Iron tools, like axes, let farmers clear more land. Iron plows made farming easier. More crops meant more people could be fed. This led to the growth of towns and cities.

Iron weapons were stronger than bronze weapons. They also had sharper edges.

Armies with iron weapons could defeat armies with bronze weapons.

THE USES OF IRON

▲ In the past, workers used ladles to pour 3,000°F (1,649°C) molten iron into molds to make cast iron.

HISTORICAL PERSPECTIVE

For thousands of years, blacksmiths made iron tools and weapons by hand. In the United States, these craftsmen produced most of the iron goods people needed. In 1890, there were over 200,000 blacksmiths in the United States. Only about sixty of them were women.

Today, many blacksmiths work in living museums. Others work shoeing horses. Some make iron works of art.

CHAPTER 3

▲ This 19th century engraving shows a factory where iron was made.

The Power of Coal

Ironworkers made their fires in a furnace. For centuries, ironworkers burned charcoal in their furnaces. As the need for iron grew, furnaces grew larger and hotter. Then a new kind of furnace was invented. It was called a blast furnace. It used more charcoal than ever before. In the early 1700s, blast furnaces began using coke. Coke is partly burned coal. With coke, furnaces could easily melt iron and make cast iron.

Today, we use iron and iron ore in many ways. We use iron to make magnets and auto parts. We use iron in medical devices. Iron is found in many different items. You can find iron in paints, inks, and dyes. You can find iron in plastics, make-up, and fertilizer, too.

THE USES OF IRON

About ninety-eight percent of iron ore is used to make steel. Steel is very important. Read on to find out why.

Processing Iron

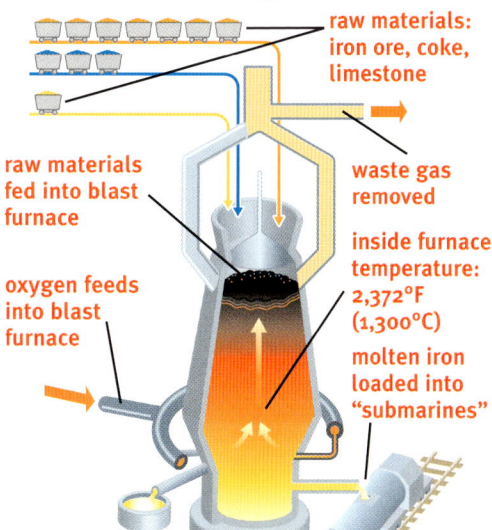

▶ Modern blast furnaces make iron from the raw materials of iron ore, limestone, and coke (coal).

THEY MADE A DIFFERENCE

Gustave Eiffel was a French engineer and builder. His specialty was making large metal buildings. He designed the Eiffel Tower for the Paris World Fair of 1889. Eiffel was one of the first builders to study the effects of wind on tall structures. His tower allows the wind to blow freely through its beams. The designs he used helped lead the way toward modern skyscrapers.

Iron and Steel

The Importance of Carbon

Carbon is an element. The symbol for carbon is C. You may know of two forms of carbon.

Diamonds are a hard form of carbon. Graphite (GRA-fite) is a soft form of carbon. The lead in your pencil is graphite.

When you melt iron ore, carbon from the burning fire becomes part of the iron. The added carbon changes the properties of iron. Too much carbon makes a metal that breaks easily. Too little carbon makes a soft iron that is easy to bend.

▲ diamond

▼ graphite

▲ Graphite and diamonds are both forms of carbon. But they have very different properties. Diamonds are the hardest minerals on Earth. Graphite is very soft.

Useable iron should be about one to three percent carbon. In the past, ironworkers knew how to make the right kind of iron. However, they did not understand how carbon changed the iron. If they got the carbon content right, they made very good iron. This iron did not shatter or bend. It was much stronger than bronze. It was even stronger than wrought iron. It would last hundreds of years. Today, we know this form of iron as steel.

Carbon Content of Iron and Steel

Substance	Amount of Carbon (percent)
Iron ore	5%
Cast iron	2–4.5%
Steel	Less than 2%
Wrought iron	Less than 1%

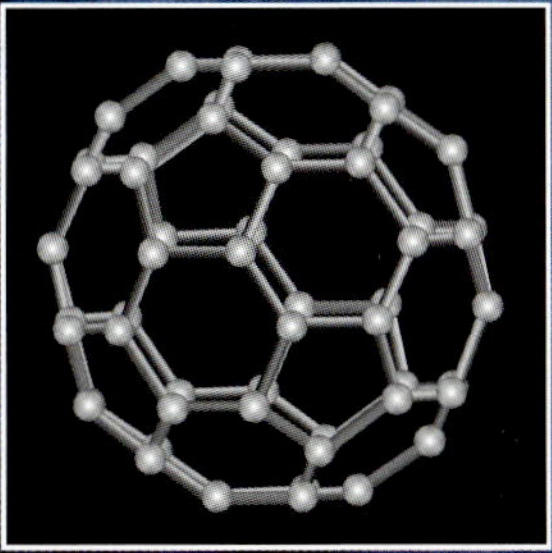

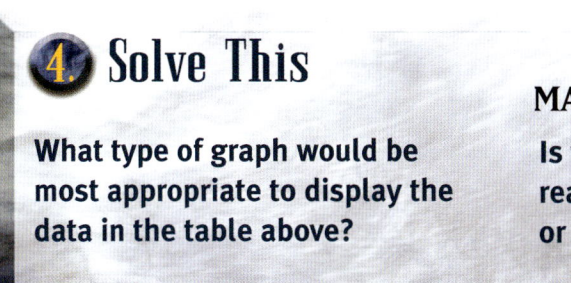
▲ steel carbon

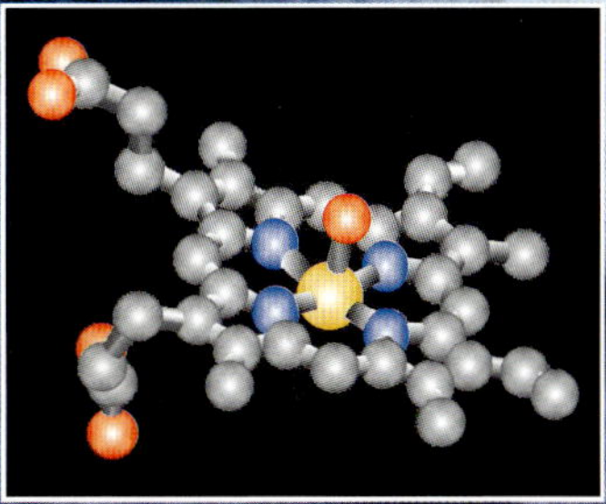

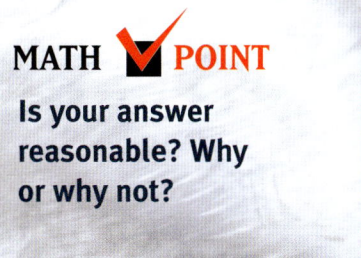
▲ iron carbon

4. Solve This

What type of graph would be most appropriate to display the data in the table above?

MATH ✓ POINT

Is your answer reasonable? Why or why not?

23

CHAPTER 4

HISTORICAL PERSPECTIVE

Historians think the first people who made steel were the Haya people of Africa. The Haya lived in what is now the country of Tanzania. These early steelmakers built clay kilns, or ovens, to heat the iron ore. The kilns were made from termite mounds. Several men sat around the kiln and used hand pumps to add air. The air made the charcoal fire burn very hot. The Haya created first-rate steel for nearly 2,000 years. Today, giant furnaces make huge amounts of steel in a short amount of time. Steelmakers rely on exact scientific formulas and computerized equipment.

The Age of Steel

Steel is made mostly from iron. Special furnaces are used to make the iron pure. The furnaces add exact amounts of other elements. They also control the amount of carbon in the iron.

Today, scientists and engineers use special **formulas** (FOR-myuh-luhz), or recipes. Making steel is like cooking. The formulas allow people to control the process.

IRON AND STEEL

The Age of Steel began in the mid-1800s. Before the 1800s, steel was very hard to make. It took a lot of time and effort to make just a little steel. This made it too costly to use. Then one man solved the problem. His name was Henry Bessemer. In 1856, he invented a new kind of furnace. The furnace was called the Bessemer Converter.

The new furnace changed steelmaking. The furnace could turn thirty tons of iron into steel in only twenty minutes. Steel could be made quickly and cheaply. In 1870, the world's yearly steel production was 500,000 tons. By 1900, it was 28 million tons per year. Steel replaced both wrought iron and cast iron. It was the ideal building material.

5. Solve This

If the Bessemer Converter could turn 30 tons of iron into steel in only 20 minutes, how many tons of iron could it convert in a 7-hour day?

MATH ✓ POINT

What steps did you use to solve this problem?

▲ Bessemer's invention was a new type of furnace. It "cooked" the iron until the metal became molten.

CHAPTER 4

Eyewitness Account

Steel has three main types: mild steel, medium steel, and tool steel. Each type has a different formula. Each type also has a different purpose. The more carbon steel has, the stronger the steel is. But high-carbon steel is also more brittle, or breakable.

Mild steel has about 0.25 percent carbon. Bridges, ships, water pipes, and cars have mild steel in them. Beams for skyscrapers are made of medium steel. Medium steel has about 0.5 percent carbon. Gears, motors, and pumps all contain medium steel.

The men who build skyscrapers balance on steel beams high above the ground. For over 100 years, Mohawk Indian ironworkers have helped build the skyscrapers in New York City. In the 1960s, they worked on the World Trade Center. Randy Horn, a Mohawk, remembers what it was like: "All of a sudden, the wind picks up and you try to balance yourself. You would have to jump from the top of the beam to the bottom of the beam and grab the top and hold on . . . and when the wind dies down, you get back up again and keep going."

IRON AND STEEL

Tool steel is a high-carbon steel. It is about 1.5 percent carbon. We use tool steel to make tools for cutting and drilling. High-carbon steel also has the largest amounts of added elements.

What about stainless steel? This type of steel has a 0.15 percent carbon content. It is made with chromium (about 18 percent) and nickel (about 8–10 percent). Chromium makes the steel rustproof. Stainless steel is used to make cooking utensils and buildings.

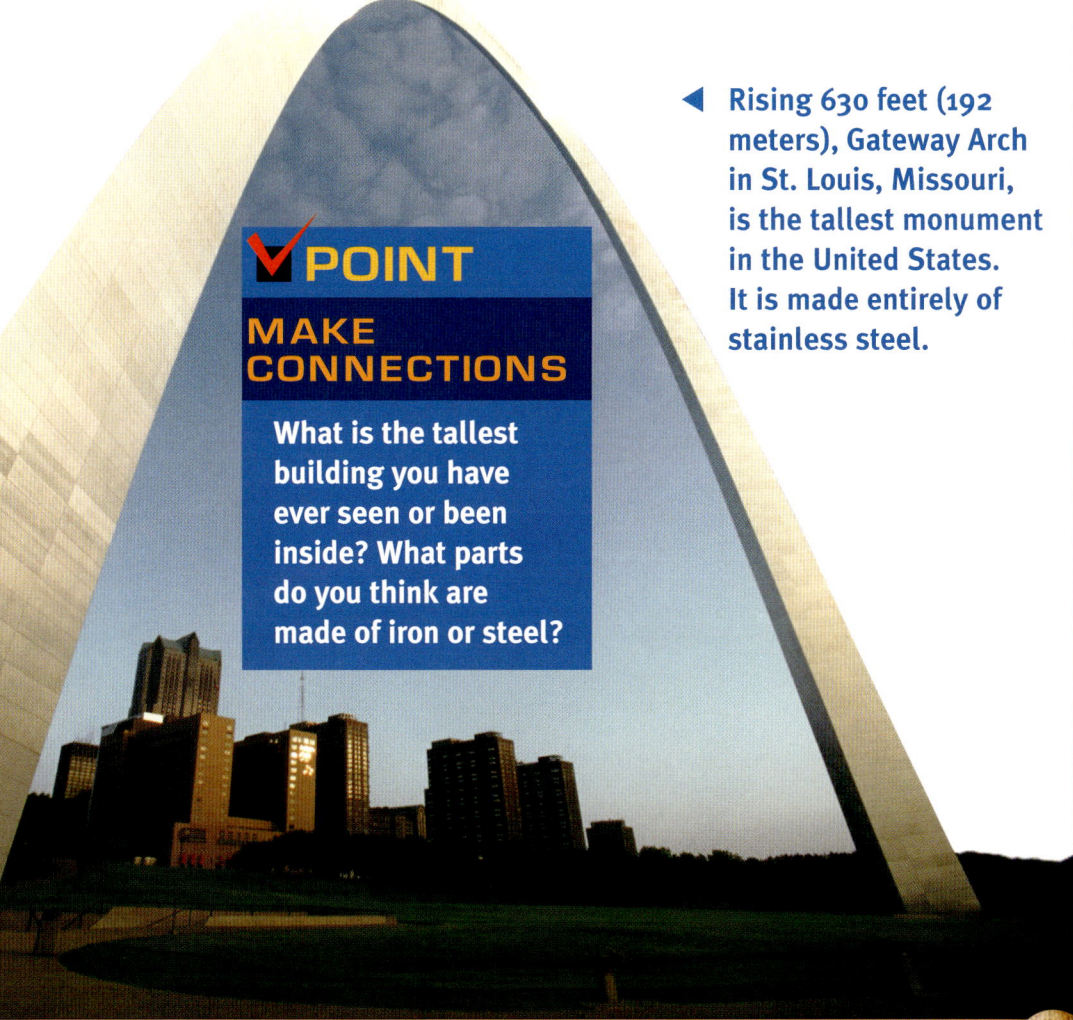

◀ Rising 630 feet (192 meters), Gateway Arch in St. Louis, Missouri, is the tallest monument in the United States. It is made entirely of stainless steel.

✓POINT
MAKE CONNECTIONS

What is the tallest building you have ever seen or been inside? What parts do you think are made of iron or steel?

CHAPTER 4

Steelmaking Today

The process of making steel has come a long way. Steelmaking today is a multi-billion-dollar industry.

1

▲ In a modern steel plant, molten steel is poured into huge molds.

2

▲ Once the steel has cooled, it is sent to rolling mills. Giant rollers reshape the steel into thick slabs or long flat sheets that can be rolled.

3

▲ Flatbed trucks carry the slabs and sheets to other factories. The factories convert the steel into many different products.

4

▲ Steelmaking keeps us supplied with many of the things we use every day.

Conclusion

At one time, people thought iron was rare. It was like gold or silver. Today, we know that iron is one of the most common elements on Earth. It can be found in many places.

Iron has special properties. Iron is a magnetic metal. It can also form compounds easily.

The first ironworkers made wrought iron. Then they learned how to make cast iron. In time, they learned how carbon changed iron. They built better furnaces. For the first time, ironworkers could make iron into steel.

Scientists work with iron to make it into stronger and lighter compounds. New ideas still improve the way steel is made. In the future, people may live on Mars and make iron products there.

Solve This Answers

1. **Page 10**
   The total thickness of the mantle, outer core, and inner core is 3,946 miles (6,350 kilometers)

2. **Page 12**
   Circumference equals diameter x pi (3.14).
   80 feet x 3.14 = 251.2 feet (24.4 meters x 3.14 = 76.6 meters)

3. **Page 16**
   Lead has the lowest melting point of the metals shown in this table. Iron has the highest melting point. Graphs should show a gradually rising line. As the rounding increases, the line will shift from gradually rising to horizontal.

4. **Page 23**
   A bar or line graph is most appropriate.

5. **Page 25**
   Step 1: 30 tons can be converted in 20 minutes, so 90 tons can be converted in 60 minutes or 1 hour. 60/20 = 3. 30 x 3 = 90
   Step 2: How much could the Bessemer Converter convert in a 7-hour day?
   90 tons x 7 hours = 630 tons